W9-BXE-681

Building a Website

ALEXA KURZIUS

Children's Press®
An Imprint of Scholastic Inc.

Content Consultant

Sarah Otts, Scratch Online Community Developer, MIT Media Lab

Library of Congress Cataloging-in-Publication Data
Names: Kurzius, Alexa, author.
Title: Building a website / by Alexa Kurzius.
Description: New York, NY : Children's Press, an imprint of Scholastic Inc., [2019] | Series: A true book | Includes bibliographical references and index.
Identifiers: LCCN 2018028048| ISBN 9780531127322 (library binding : alk. paper) | ISBN 9780531135419 (pbk. : alk. paper)
Subjects: LCSH: Web site development—Juvenile literature. | Web sites—Design—Juvenile literature.
Classification: LCC TK5105.888 .K87 2019 | DDC 006.7—dc23
LC record available at https://lccn.loc.gov/2018028048

All rights reserved. Published in 2019 by Children's Press, an imprint of Scholastic Inc.
Printed in North Mankato, MN, USA 113

SCHOLASTIC, CHILDREN'S PRESS, A TRUE BOOK™, and associated logos are trademarks and/or registered trademarks of Scholastic Inc.

Scholastic Inc., 557 Broadway, New York, NY 10012

1 2 3 4 5 6 7 8 9 10 R 28 27 26 25 24 23 22 21 20 19

Front: Web designers
Back: Web users

Find the Truth!

Everything you are about to read is true *except* for one of the sentences on this page.

Which one is **TRUE**?

T or F The World Wide Web is just one part of the internet.

T or F Websites have been around for more than 100 years.

Find the answers in this book.

Contents

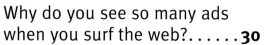

THE **BIG** TRUTH!

Big Business

J.C.R. Licklider (left)
came up with the idea
for the internet.

Web developers

4 Getting Noticed

This is Nadia. Help her build a website on page 40 and fix another one on page 42!

There are almost 300 million internet users in the United States and about three billion worldwide.

The internet makes it easy for information to spread among huge groups of people.

CHAPTER **1**

Getting Connected

People today have more information at their fingertips than ever before. This is because of the internet, a system of thousands of connected computer **networks**. The internet has revolutionized how we communicate. It allows information to be transmitted almost instantly to anyone in the world. The internet has only been in widespread use since the 1990s. It is constantly changing as technology improves and the world becomes more connected.

1950s

Today

The smartphones many people carry every day are far more powerful than older computers that once filled entire rooms.

Computer History

Computer technology has changed a lot in the last 75 years. The first electronic computers were giant calculators that could solve complex math problems. They were the size of an entire room and weighed thousands of pounds! At first, they were only used by researchers at universities and by the military. But in the 1950s, many businesses began installing computers in their offices.

An Intergalactic Network

Early computers could not communicate with each other the way they do today. But beginning in the 1960s, researchers began considering the idea that computers could be connected and exchange information with each other. J.C.R. Licklider, a professor at the Massachusetts Institute of Technology (MIT), was the first to come up with the idea of the internet. He called it an "intergalactic network." In 1962, Licklider took a job at the U.S. government's Advanced Research Projects Agency. There, he worked with others to advance his ideas about computer networks.

J.C.R. Licklider (left) assists a student while teaching at MIT.

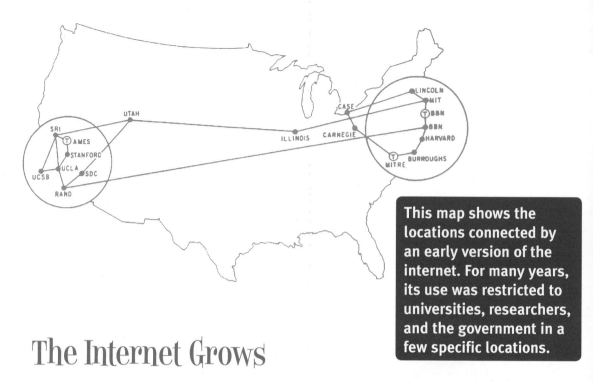

This map shows the locations connected by an early version of the internet. For many years, its use was restricted to universities, researchers, and the government in a few specific locations.

The Internet Grows

Between the 1960s and 1980s, computer scientists worked to develop the first computer networks. During the same time, computers got smaller and more powerful. Many people began using them at home. In 1969, researchers in California used cables to connect two computers together. Then they connected even more computers to create networks. Finally, they connected these networks together. This was the earliest version of the internet.

In 1989, British scientist Tim Berners-Lee came up with the idea of the World Wide Web, or simply "web," a way of making it easy for people to share and view information on the internet. Before the web, using the internet was complicated. It was especially hard to go from one file to another without knowing the exact address of what you were looking for. Web users could post pages of text, photos, and other content online. Then others could access these web pages using a **browser**. Users could jump from one web page to another by clicking on links. Berners-Lee called these links "hypertext."

The British royal family launched its official website in 1997. At the time, it looked like this.

The Internet Age

The number of internet users grew very quickly in the 1990s. Many people who had never owned computers began purchasing them so they could go online at home. In 1994, 11 million Americans had internet access in their households. By the end of the decade, the number had risen to more than 121 million. 😃

One of the earliest known items to be purchased online was a Pizza Hut pepperoni pizza in 1994. 😎

In 1995, there were fewer than 500,000 computers in all U.S. public schools with internet access. By 2005, there were more than 12 million!

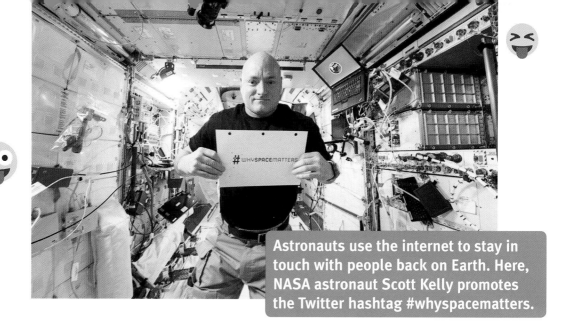

Astronauts use the internet to stay in touch with people back on Earth. Here, NASA astronaut Scott Kelly promotes the Twitter hashtag #whyspacematters.

Today, we live in a world where many people are online all the time. The internet can be accessed using computers of all shapes and sizes, from smartphones and wearable devices to traditional desktops and laptops. Most people use wireless internet, also called Wi-Fi, which enables them to connect to the internet without any cables. Wi-Fi access has even been brought to some very remote locations. In 2010, it was introduced to Mount Everest—the highest mountain in the world—and the International Space Station in outer space!

U.S. internet users spend more than $450 billion per year shopping online.

Online stores are some of the most popular websites today.

14

CHAPTER 2

Website Basics

Every day, we use a huge variety of information to learn, make decisions, and solve problems. Much of the information we get comes from websites. A website is a collection of web pages that are linked together under the same **domain name**. Do you want to find out which team won last night's basketball game? Check whether it might rain tomorrow? Do research for a school project? There are websites for all this and much more.

Suffix	What it means	What kind of websites use it
.edu	Education	Websites run by schools
.com	Commercial	Websites run by businesses
.org	Organization	Websites run by groups like charities, environmental groups, or community clubs
.gov	Government	A U.S. government website
.mil	Military	A U.S. military branch's website

All domain names have a suffix. Suffixes help explain what kind of website the domain contains. Here are some of the most common suffixes.

Getting to a Website

Websites are accessed using programs called web browsers. Web browsers allow people to look through—or browse—the World Wide Web. Google Chrome, Microsoft Edge, Safari, and Firefox are some of the most popular browsers. Web **developers** test their sites in multiple browsers to make sure they work correctly for everyone.

Understanding Web Addresses

Web browsers have a place to type in a Uniform Resource Locator, or URL. This is a website's address. Each URL has several parts. Entering a simple domain name and suffix will usually take you to a website's home page. Other pages on the site might have longer URLs. Check out these examples:

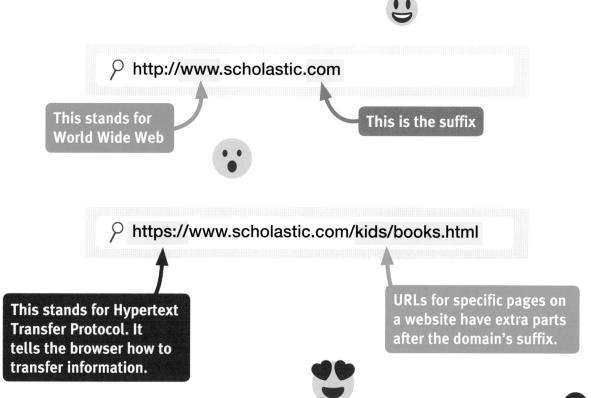

http://www.scholastic.com

This stands for World Wide Web

This is the suffix

https://www.scholastic.com/kids/books.html

This stands for Hypertext Transfer Protocol. It tells the browser how to transfer information.

URLs for specific pages on a website have extra parts after the domain's suffix.

The world's largest data center covers more than 10 million square feet (929,030 square meters). That is more than 173 football fields!

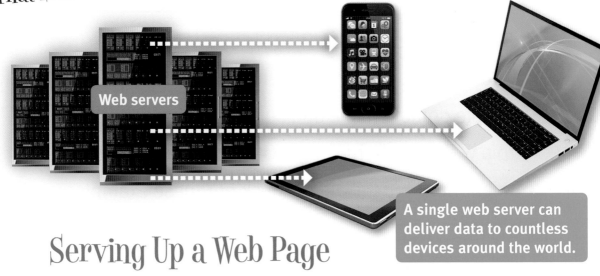

Web servers

A single web server can deliver data to countless devices around the world.

Serving Up a Web Page

All websites are hosted on **servers**. Servers are computers that exist to provide files to other computers. Typing a URL into a web browser connects your computer to a server. Then your computer downloads the files needed to display the web page on your screen.

Most websites are hosted at **data** centers. These are huge rooms or buildings filled with stacks and stacks of servers.

Web Hosting Companies

You don't need your own server to make a website. Most people or businesses with websites hire web hosting companies to provide server space. Web hosting companies also help users register domain names. Users upload the files for their websites and post the files to the hosting company's servers. Then people around the world can access the site.

In data centers, huge racks of servers fill enormous rooms.

Parts of a Website

Each website has different parts. The home page is the first page you see. It is the main page of the website. Other web pages are linked to the home page. There might be a menu of links along the top, bottom, or side of the page. This is called a navigation bar. A header is at the top of most web pages. This usually tells you the name of the website. Below the header is the page's body content. This could be text, photos, video, or anything else you would view on a web page.

Most websites are made up of many linked pages. A news website might be organized something like this, for example.

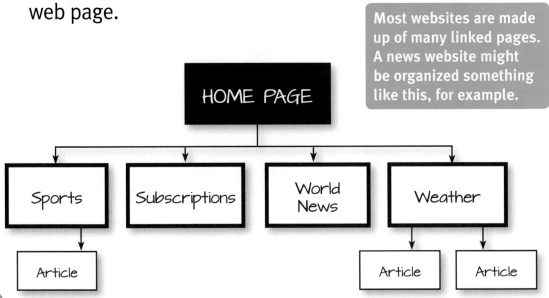

Header

Navigation bar

Body content

https://www.myneighborhoodnews.org

My Neighborhood News   Home   News   Services   Contact   SEARCH

A shark has been spotted at our beach!

Links to other pages on the website

Fifth graders visit   Schools celebrates   This week's

The home page of a news website might look something like this.

The look of a website's home page can tell you a lot about the site's purpose. News websites have articles to read or videos to watch just below the header. Email websites display new and old messages in an inbox. A video streaming website might show a list of popular or recent videos. Social media sites show a mixture of messages, photos, videos, and links that users post.

Web developers often work in teams. Each member often specializes in a certain part of creating a website. 😎

More than 162,900 people work as web developers in the United States.

⭐ **3**

😃

Designing a Website

People all over the world need websites to help run their businesses, share information, and connect with others. But not everyone has the skills or knowledge to create their own sites. Instead, they often hire web developers to get the job done. Web developers write the **code** that makes the site work. Code is a set of instructions that tells a computer what to do. It is written using a variety of programming languages.

😍

HTML:

```
<a href= "https://www.scholastic.com/kids/books.html">
Check out this cool link!</a>
```

This code creates a link on a page.

CSS:

```
body {
    background-color: red;
    }
```

This code makes the background of the main part of a web page red.

Learning New Languages

Web developers rely on a number of different coding languages. Some of the most common ones are HTML (hypertext markup language), CSS (cascading style sheets), and JavaScript. HTML gives web pages their basic structure. CSS is used to modify colors, **fonts**, and other things that affect the look of a web page. JavaScript is used to create interactive parts of a web page, such as forms that need to be filled out.

HTML is the backbone of web design. It is the first language most web developers learn to use. It works by labeling text with tags. These tags tell the computer what to do with any text that is placed inside of them. With HTML, you can add images, sound, and video to a web page. You can also change the basic look of the page and add links to connect multiple pages together.

Once you learn the basics of HTML, you'll have all the skills you need to create simple websites.

```
<!DOCTYPE html PUBLIC "-//W
<html xmlns="http://www.w3.
  <head>
    <meta http-equiv="Conte
    <meta http-equiv="Conte
    <meta http-equiv="Conte
    <title>Document Title</
    <link rev="made" href="
    <link rev="start" href=
    <style type="text/css"
```

All About Tags

Most tags have two parts: a start and an end. However, some tags only have one part. Here are some of the most common ones:

Start tag	Definition	End tag	Definition
<html>	Starts an HTML document	</html>	Ends an HTML document
<title>	Creates the website title for the web browser	</title>	Ends the website title for the web browser
<body>	Starts where the content (text, links, images, and more) goes on your web page	</body>	Ends the content on your web page
<h1>	Start tag for text with the largest size. The h stands for "header." Text tags go from largest to smallest in size from <h1>, <h2>, <h3>, and so on.	</h1>	End tag for text with the largest size
<img src=" "/>	Start and end tag for an image. You put the web address for the image between the quotation marks.		
<a href= "URL">	Start tag for a link. Put the real web address between the quotation marks. After the tag, type the text you want to be linked.	</a>	End tag for a link

From Code to Content

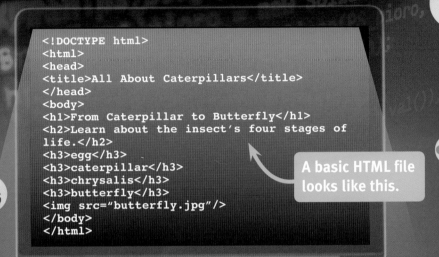

```
<!DOCTYPE html>
<html>
<head>
<title>All About Caterpillars</title>
</head>
<body>
<h1>From Caterpillar to Butterfly</h1>
<h2>Learn about the insect's four stages of
life.</h2>
<h3>egg</h3>
<h3>caterpillar</h3>
<h3>chrysalis</h3>
<h3>butterfly</h3>
<img src="butterfly.jpg"/>
</body>
</html>
```

A basic HTML file looks like this.

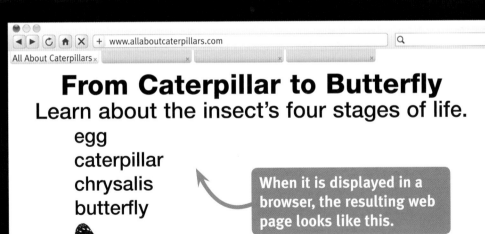

www.allaboutcaterpillars.com

All About Caterpillars

From Caterpillar to Butterfly
Learn about the insect's four stages of life.
egg
caterpillar
chrysalis
butterfly

When it is displayed in a browser, the resulting web page looks like this.

Start by brainstorming ideas!

Making Your Own Website

If you want to make your own website, start with these basic steps:

1 **Come up with an idea:** Think about what your website will look like, how it will work, and which kinds of information it will contain.

2 **Register a domain name and purchase server space:** Come up with a domain name and register it with a web hosting company.

3 **Choose how you want to work:** You can build a website from scratch using code or try a **template**.

4 **Build and test:** Add content to your website. If you're using a template, add and edit your pages. If you're building your site from scratch, upload your HTML files. Check to see how the site looks in different browsers. Look for **bugs**, or errors, in your website and fix them.

Do plenty of research.

5 **Ask for help:** If you get stuck, talk to your teachers, family, and friends. Or try using Google to search for a solution to your problem.

6 **Spread the word:** Share your finished website with friends and family.

Have fun!

Big Business

Businesses need customers to buy goods or services. This helps the business make money. Advertisements, or ads, tell people about the goods or services that a company sells. Today, many websites are run by businesses.

There are also many sites that make money solely through hosting advertisements. Online advertisements are a convenient way for these websites to find new customers. There are many different types of online ads. Check them out!

Banner ads are images that often link to another website.

When you Google a word or phrase, often the first result is an advertisement. You'll see a label that says "ad."

Pop-up ads are like banner ads, but they "pop up" on screen to cover the website you're visiting. Some pop-up ads are videos. They are similar to TV commercials.

People around the world make billions of Google searches every day.

What are you searching for?

Searching online is one of the fastest ways to gather information and answer questions.

CHAPTER **4**

Getting Noticed

The internet is kind of like the world's largest library. But instead of books, there are billions of web pages to browse through. Together, they contain information on just about any topic anyone could imagine. So how do you find the exact website you need when you're looking for specific information? Search engines are a big help. These websites organize and sort through information online so it is easier to track down what you need.

Search results are usually ordered based on how well they match your search terms and how popular they are.

How Search Engines Work

Google is the most-used search engine worldwide. It uses programs called spiders to find as many web pages as they can on the internet. Spiders work by following links on pages to other pages. They gather their results in a list called a search index. When you use Google, you type in words or phrases. Google then looks through its search index to see if it can find web pages that match your search terms. Finally, it gives you a list of links.

Metadata

Metadata is data that describes other data. Web developers add metadata to web pages as part of the coding process. This metadata is invisible when looking at the page in a browser, but it provides useful information to some search engines. Metadata includes a list of words people might use if they are searching for the information listed on the website. Imagine you have a website about making a birthday cake. You might add these terms to your metadata:

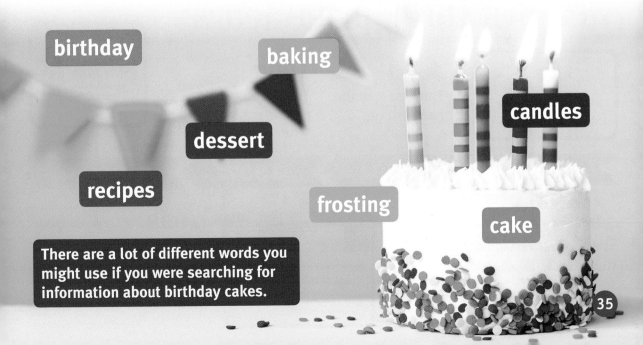

birthday

baking

candles

dessert

recipes

frosting

cake

There are a lot of different words you might use if you were searching for information about birthday cakes.

A Different Kind of Cookie

Many websites track your activity using something called cookies. Cookies are small files that a server sends to a user's web browser. They help identify who is using the website. For example, cookies can keep you logged in to a website or help an online store keep track of what's in your shopping cart. Companies can also use cookies to track how you use a website.

Websites Through the Years

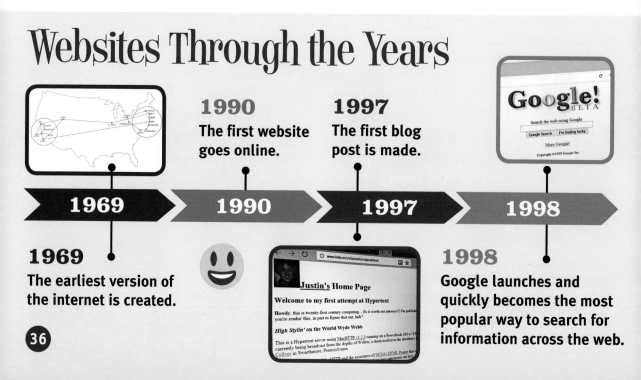

1990
The first website goes online.

1997
The first blog post is made.

1969 → 1990 → 1997 → 1998

1969
The earliest version of the internet is created.

1998
Google launches and quickly becomes the most popular way to search for information across the web.

Getting Personal

Many websites make you create your own account with a username and password. This lets you store information on the website you can use later. When creating a password, remember to avoid using an obvious word or phrase that someone might be able to guess. If you don't have a good password, **hackers** might sneak into your account to steal your personal information.

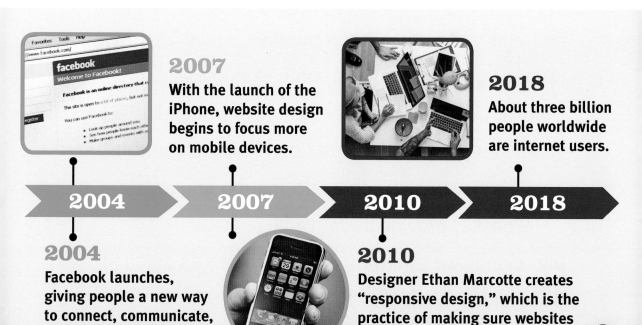

2007
With the launch of the iPhone, website design begins to focus more on mobile devices.

2018
About three billion people worldwide are internet users.

2004 | **2007** | **2010** | **2018**

2004
Facebook launches, giving people a new way to connect, communicate, and keep track of others.

2010
Designer Ethan Marcotte creates "responsive design," which is the practice of making sure websites can work on any device.

Remember to take breaks from websites and your devices. It's good for your brain!

The Importance of Privacy

Certain information is yours and yours alone. Your first and last name, phone number, Social Security number, and birthday are some examples. Unfortunately, there are people who will try to steal your personal information. Be extra cautious about how you share this information online.

Websites provide us with a huge amount of information we use every day. But there's so much to discover in real life too! 😃

Staying Safe

Follow these tips to help stay safe online:

1. **Use trusted websites:** Stick to websites and apps that a parent or trusted adult approves of.
   - Keep your identity private: Don't share personal info or post photos and videos without permission from a parent or trusted adult.

2. **Store passwords safely:** Don't share your passwords with other people.

3. **Think before you click:**

   - Don't post photos or videos that you might regret later or that might hurt someone's feelings. They can stay online forever.

   - Don't click links or open files from people you don't trust.

   - Don't buy things online without permission from a parent or trusted adult.

   - If someone you meet online asks for personal information or wants to meet in person, tell a trusted adult immediately. Not everyone online tells the truth about who they are.

Storyboarding a Website

Before building a website, you need a plan. You need to create a storyboard, or sketch, of your website. Imagine you are creating a website about your favorite animal. Create a storyboard for your website. Make sure the site gives your visitors all the information they might want to learn about the animal.

Materials

- ◯ Plain paper or graph paper
- ◯ Pencil

What should I include in my website about pandas?

Steps:

1. Make a list of information you might want to include on your site.

   - Name of animal
   - What the animal eats
   - Where it lives
   - What threats it faces in the wild
   - Photos, videos, or sound recordings of the animal
   - Links to pages that offer even more information

2. Draw a picture of what your website's home page would look like.

3. Draw arrows from it to the other pages on the website. For example, you might have a separate page for information about baby animals. You might have another page for information about the animal's lifestyle.

Web Site Design
Home Page

All About Pandas

Menu

Main content

Debugging Challenge

A student made a web page about basketball. She wanted the following information to appear in order on the web page:
- A header that says Get Ready to Play Basketball
- Body copy that says "Learn what equipment you need to play this sport."
- Four headers about the basic equipment kids need to play the sport. (Basketball, Hoop, Court, Sneakers)
- An image of a basketball

Find the student's mistakes in the code below and fix them. This is called debugging. Check page 26 to learn more about HTML tags.

```
<!DOCTYPE html>
<html>

<img src="baseball.jpg"/>
<body>Image of a basketball</body>

<h3>Basketball</h3><h4>Hoop</h4><h3>Court</h3>
<h3>Sneakers</h3>

<head>
<title>Get Ready to Play Basketball</title>
</head>
<body>
<h1>Get Ready to Play Basketball</h1>

<body>Learn what equipment you need to play this
sport.</body>

</html>
```

Can you help Nadia debug the code she wrote?

Basketball
Hoop

Court

Sneakers

Get Ready to Play Basketball

Learn what equipment you need to play this sport.

Answers: The list of four <h3> headers should be positioned under the body text.; The image URL is wrong. It should be a basketball.; The tags around "hoop" are wrong. This makes it the wrong size.

43

True Statistics

Number of internet users in the United States: About 300 million

Number of internet users worldwide: About 3 billion

Percentage of U.S. kids who have their own digital device by age 9: About 50

Number of active websites on the internet today: About 200 million

Did you find the truth?

(T) The World Wide Web is just one part of the internet.

(F) Websites have been around for more than 100 years.

Resources

Books

Lyons, Heather. *Coding in the Real World*. Minneapolis: Lerner Publications, 2018.

Lyons, Heather. *Coding to Create and Communicate*. Minneapolis: Lerner Publications, 2018.

Lyons, Heather. *Programming Games and Animation*. Minneapolis: Lerner Publications, 2018.

Wainewright, Max. *How to Code: A Step-by-Step Guide to Computer Coding*. New York: Sterling Children's Books, 2016.

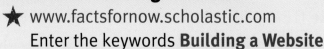

Visit this Scholastic website for more information on building a website:
★ www.factsfornow.scholastic.com
Enter the keywords **Building a Website**

Important Words

browser (BROW-zur) a computer program that lets you find and look at web pages or other data

bugs (BUHGZ) errors in a computer program or system

code (KODE) the instructions of a computer program, written in a programming language

data (DAY-tuh) information collected in a place so that something can be done with it

developers (dih-VEL-uh-purz) people who work to create websites or computer programs

domain name (doh-MAYN NAYM) a general address on the World Wide Web, such as scholastic.com or whitehouse.gov

fonts (FAHNTS) styles of type

hackers (HAK-urz) people who have special skills for getting into computer systems without permission

networks (NET-wurks) groups of connected computers or communications equipment

servers (SUR-vurz) computers shared by two or more users in a network

template (TEM-plit) a document or pattern that is used to create similar documents

Index

Page numbers in **bold** indicate illustrations.

About the Author

Alexa Kurzius writes and produces videos for Scholastic's elementary STEM magazines. She's been reporting ever since the fourth grade, when she penned a picture book about penguins. She has an undergraduate degree in English and psychology and a master's degree in science journalism. She lives in New York City with her husband.